Highland Cows

Meet Lulu and Cooper

Lulu and Cooper are best friends. They enjoy spending their days playing in the fields, grazing in the sun, and going on mischievous adventures together. They live on a farm in the South and come running when they hear their farmer calling from the gate with special treats.

Originating from the Scottish Highlands, these majestic and beautiful animals are one of the world's oldest breeds. Their long wooly coats keep them warm in the colder climates and their ability to thrive in tough conditions make them extremely resilient.

With their wild windswept hair, gentle personality, and their ability to overcome odds that others would not, Highland cows have become a symbol of enduring strength, natural beauty, and true kindness. They have captured the hearts of many, including our designers here at Leisure Arts. We hope you enjoy crafting these handsome projects as much as we have enjoyed creating them. May they bring peace, conversation, and loving kinship to all who adore them.

HIGHLAND COW

INTERMEDIATE

Finished Measurements

Length: 9" (23 cm)

Height: 8" (20.5 cm)

SHOPPING LIST

Yarn (Medium Weight) 

[3.5 ounces, 185 yards (100 grams, 170 meters) per skein]:

- ☐ Main Color (Brown) - 1 skein
- ☐ Dark Brown - 1 skein **or** 23 yards (21 meters)
- ☐ Cream - 1 skein **or** 22 yards (20 meters)

Crochet Hook

- ☐ Size G (4 mm) **or** size needed for gauge

Additional Supplies

- ☐ 12 mm Safety eyes - 2
- ☐ Polyester fiberfill
- ☐ Yarn needle

GAUGE INFORMATION

16 sc and 18 rows/rnds = 4" (10 cm)

Gauge Swatch: 4" (5 cm) square

With Main Color, ch 9.

Row 1: Sc in second ch from hook and in each ch across: 8 sc.

Rows 2-18: Ch 1, turn; sc in each sc across.

Finish off.

Save time, check your gauge.

STITCH GUIDE

SINGLE CROCHET 2 TOGETHER

(abbreviated sc2tog)

Pull up a loop in each of next 2 sts, YO and draw through all 3 loops on hook ***(Fig. A)*** **(counts as one sc)**.

Fig. A

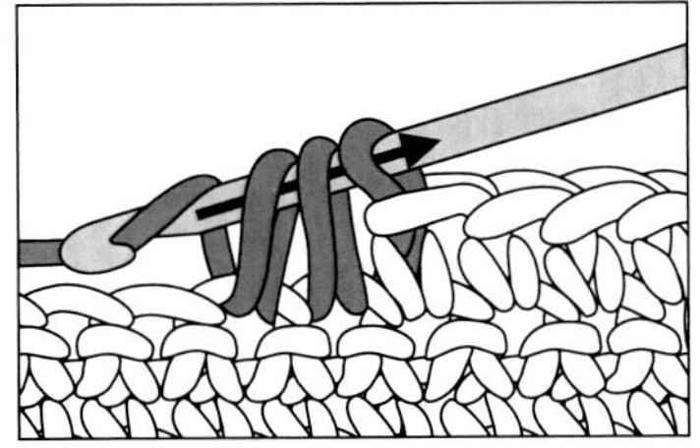

PATTERN NOTES

Cow is made in sections: Legs, Belly, Body, Head, Ears, and Horns. Hair is added last to sections like fringe. When stuffing with polyester fiberfill, do not add so much that stitches stretch and fiberfill shows between stitches.

LEG (Make 4)

Rnd 1 (Right side)**:** With Dark Brown, ch 2, 6 sc in second ch from hook; join with slip st to first sc.

Note: Loop a short piece of yarn around any stitch to mark Rnd 1 as **right** side.

Rnd 2: Ch 1, 2 sc in same st as joining and in each sc around; join with slip st to first sc: 12 sc.

Rnd 3: Ch 1, working in the Back Loops Only ***(Fig. 4, page 40)***, sc in same st as joining and in each sc around; join with slip st to **both** loops of first sc.

Rnds 4-6: Ch 1, working in both loops, sc in same st as joining and in each sc around; join with slip st to first sc.

Finish off.

Rnd 7: With **right** side facing, join Main Color with slip st in same st as joining; ch 1, sc in same st and in each sc around; join with slip st to first sc.

Rnds 8-10: Ch 1, sc in same st as joining and in each sc around; join with slip st to first sc.

Rnd 11: Ch 1, working in Back Loops Only, sc in same st as joining and in next 4 sc, 2 sc in next sc, sc in next 5 sc, 2 sc in next sc; join with slip st to **both** loops of first sc: 14 sc.

Note: When working in the Back Loops Only here and in the Body section, it will leave the Front Loop exposed. The front loop will be used when adding the Hair to the Legs and Body after the Cow has been completed.

Rnd 12: Ch 1, working in both loops, sc in same st as joining and in next 5 sc, 2 sc in next sc, sc in next 6 sc, 2 sc in next sc; join with slip st to first sc: 16 sc.

Rnd 13: Ch 1, sc in same st as joining and in next 2 sc, 2 sc in next sc, ★ sc in next 3 sc, 2 sc in next sc; repeat from ★ around; join with slip st to first sc: 20 sc.

Rnd 14: Ch 1, sc in same st as joining and in next 2 sc, 2 sc in next sc, ★ sc in next 3 sc, 2 sc in next sc; repeat from ★ around; join with slip st to first sc: 25 sc.

Finish off 3 of the Legs (do **not** finish off the fourth Leg).

Stuff Leg with polyester fiberfill.

BELLY

Note: Row 1 will join an additional Leg to the Belly.

Row 1 (Right side)**:** Continuing with fourth Leg, ch 1, sc in same st as joining and in next 7 sc, leave remaining 17 sts unworked, sc in first 8 sc of next Leg, leave remaining 17 sts unworked (you will have a straight row): 16 sc.

Note: Mark Row 1 as **right** side.

Rows 2-16: Ch 1, turn; sc in each sc across.

Note: Row 17 will join the remaining Legs to the Belly.

Row 17: Ch 1, turn; holding the **right** sides of the Leg and Belly together and working through **both** sts of the Leg and Belly at the **same** time, sc in first 8 sc; working through **both** sts of the last Leg and Belly at the **same** time, sc in first 8 sc; do **not** finish off: 16 sc.

Note: The joining sc seam on Row 17 will be raised on the **wrong** side.

BODY

Rnd 1 (Right side)**:** Ch 1, ★ sc in end of next 16 rows across Belly, sc in next 12 sc on next Leg leaving last 5 sc unworked, skip next 5 sc on next Leg, sc in next 12 sc on Leg (this will give you a straight line across); repeat from ★ once **more**; join with slip st to first sc: 80 sc.

Note #1: Mark Rnd 1 as **right** side.

Note #2: The gaps between the Legs will be sewn together after the Body has been completed.

Rnd 2: Ch 1, working in the Back Loops Only, sc in same st as joining and in each sc around; join with slip st to **both** loops of first sc.

Rnds 3-6: Ch 1, working in both loops, sc in same st as joining and in each sc around; join with slip st to first sc.

Rnd 7: Ch 1, working in the Back Loops Only, sc in same st as joining and in next 15 sc, (sc in next 4 sc, sc2tog) 4 times, sc in next 16 sc, (sc in next 4 sc, sc2tog) 4 times; join with slip st to **both** loops of first sc: 72 sc.

Rnd 8: Ch 1, working in both loops, sc in same st as joining and in each sc around; join with slip st to first sc.

Rnd 9: Ch 1, sc in same st as joining and in next 15 sc, (sc in next 3 sc, sc2tog) 4 times, sc in next 16 sc, (sc in next 3 sc, sc2tog) 4 times; join with slip st to first sc: 64 sc.

Rnd 10: Ch 1, sc in same st as joining and in each sc around; join with slip st to first sc.

Rnd 11: Ch 1, sc in same st as joining and in next 15 sc, (sc in next 2 sc, sc2tog) 4 times, sc in next 16 sc, (sc in next 2 sc, sc2tog) 4 times; join with slip st to first sc: 56 sc.

Rnd 12: Ch 1, working in the Back Loops Only, sc in same st as joining and in each sc around; join with slip st to **both** loops of first sc.

Rnd 13: Ch 1, working in both loops, sc in same st as joining and in next 5 sc, sc2tog, sc in next 6 sc, sc2tog, (sc in next sc, sc2tog) 4 times, (sc in next 6 sc, sc2tog) twice, (sc in next sc, sc2tog) 4 times; join with slip st to first sc: 44 sc.

Rnd 14: Ch 1, sc in same st as joining and in each sc around; join with slip st to first sc.

Rnd 15: Ch 1, sc in same st as joining and in next 13 sc, sc2tog 4 times, sc in next 14 sc, sc2tog 4 times; join with slip st to first sc: 36 sc.

Rnd 16: Ch 1, sc in same st as joining and in each sc around; join with slip st to first sc, finish off leaving a 10" (25.5 cm) length for sewing.

Firmly stuff Body with polyester fiberfill.

Thread yarn needle with 10" (25.5 cm) length and sew together by using the **Back Loops Only**. This will allow the front loops to be exposed and will be used to add the Hair.

Cut an 8" (20.5 cm) length of Main Color yarn. Thread yarn needle and, working through **both** loops, sew each gap between Legs closed.

HEAD

Rnd 1 (Right side)**:** With Cream and beginning at the muzzle, ch 8; 2 sc in second ch from hook, sc in next 5 chs, 4 sc in last ch; working in free loops on opposite side of ch ***(Fig. 5b, page 40)***, sc in next 5 chs, 2 sc in next ch; join with slip st to first sc: 18 sc.

Note: Mark Rnd 1 as **right** side.

Rnd 2: Ch 1, sc in same st as joining, 2 sc in next sc, sc in next 5 sc, 2 sc in next sc, sc in next 2 sc, 2 sc in next sc, sc in next 5 sc, 2 sc in next sc, sc in last sc; join with slip st to first sc: 22 sc.

Rnd 3: Ch 1, sc in same st as joining, 2 sc in next sc, sc in next 7 sc, 2 sc in next sc, sc in next 2 sc, 2 sc in next sc, sc in next 7 sc, 2 sc in next sc, sc in last sc; join with slip st to first sc: 26 sc.

Rnd 4: Ch 1, sc in same st as joining and in next sc, 2 sc in next sc, sc in next 7 sc, 2 sc in next sc, sc in next 4 sc, 2 sc in next sc, sc in next 7 sc, 2 sc in next sc, sc in last 2 sc; join with slip st to first sc: 30 sc.

Rnds 5-7: Ch 1, sc in same st as joining and in each sc around; join with slip st to first sc.

Finish off.

Rnd 8: With **right** side facing and working in Back Loops Only, join Main Color with slip st in same st as joining; ch 1, sc in same st and in next 18 sc, 2 sc in each of next 9 sc, sc in last 2 sc; join with slip st to **both** loops of first sc: 39 sc.

Rnds 9 and 10: Ch 1, working in both loops, sc in same st as joining and in each sc around; join with slip st to first sc.

Rnd 11: Ch 1, sc in same st as joining and in next 21 sc, 2 sc in next sc, sc in next 3 sc, 2 sc in next sc, sc in next 2 sc, 2 sc in next sc, sc in next 3 sc, 2 sc in next sc, sc in last 5 sc; join with slip st to first sc: 43 sc.

Rnd 12: Ch 1, 2 sc in same st as joining, sc in next sc and in each sc around; join with slip st to first sc: 44 sc.

Rnds 13-17: Ch 1, sc in same st as joining and in each sc around; join with slip st to first sc.

Rnd 18: Ch 1, sc in same st as joining and in next 8 sc, sc2tog, ★ sc in next 9 sc, sc2tog; repeat from ★ around; join with slip st to first sc: 40 sc.

Rnd 19: Ch 1, sc in same st as joining and in next 2 sc, sc2tog, ★ sc in next 3 sc, sc2tog; repeat from ★ around; join with slip st to first sc: 32 sc.

Rnd 20: Ch 1, sc in same st as joining and in each sc around; join with slip st to first sc.

Rnd 21: Ch 1, sc in same st as joining and in next sc, sc2tog, ★ sc in next 2 sc, sc2tog; repeat from ★ around; join with slip st to first sc: 24 sc.

Rnd 22: Ch 1, sc in same st as joining, sc2tog, ★ sc in next sc, sc2tog; repeat from ★ around; join with slip st to first sc: 16 sc.

Attach safety eyes between Rnds 9 and 10 about 9 stitches apart ***(see Attaching Safety Eyes, page 40)***.

Stuff Head with polyester fiberfill.

Rnd 23: Ch 1, beginning in same st as joining, sc2tog 8 times; join with slip st to first sc: 8 sc.

Finish off leaving an 8" (20.5 cm) length for sewing.

Thread yarn needle with yarn length and weave yarn through sts on Rnd 23 to close; secure end.

HORN (Make 2)

Rnd 1 (Right side)**:** With Cream, ch 2, 3 sc in second ch from hook; do **not** join, place marker to indicate the beginning of the round ***(Fig. 1, page 39)***.

Note: Mark Rnd 1 as **right** side.

Rnd 2: Sc in each sc around: 3 sc.

Rnd 3: 2 Sc in next sc, sc in next 2 sc: 4 sc.

Rnd 4: 2 Sc in next sc, sc in next 3 sc: 5 sc.

Rnd 5: Sc in each sc around.

Rnd 6: 2 Sc in next sc, sc in next 4 sc: 6 sc.

Rnd 7: 2 Sc in next sc, sc in next 5 sc: 7 sc.

Rnd 8: 2 Sc in next sc, sc in next 6 sc: 8 sc.

Rnd 9: (2 Sc in next sc, sc in next 3 sc) twice: 10 sc.

Rnd 10: (2 Sc in next sc, sc in next 4 sc) twice: 12 sc.

Rnd 11: 2 Sc in next sc, sc in next 11 sc; slip st in next sc, finish off leaving an 8" (20.5 cm) length for sewing: 13 sts
Stuff Horn with polyester fiberfill.

Thread yarn needle with long length and sew each Horn on Head, across Rnds 16-19.

EAR (Make 2)

Row 1: With Main Color, ch 4, 8 dc in fourth ch from hook **(3 skipped chs count as first dc)**: 9 dc.

Row 2 (Right side)**:** Ch 1, turn; 2 sc in first dc and in each dc across; finish off leaving an 8" (20.5 cm) length for sewing: 18 sc.

Note: Mark Row 2 as **right** side. Thread yarn needle with long length and sew each Ear to Head below Horn, folding the Ear before sewing.

TAIL

Row 1 (Right side)**:** With Dark Brown and leaving a 6" (15 cm) length for sewing to Body, ch 8, sc in second ch from hook and in each ch across: 7 sc.

Note: Mark Row 1 as **right** side.

Rows 2 and 3: Ch 1, turn; sc in each sc across.

Finish off leaving an 8" (20.5 cm) length for sewing.

Cut 9 strands of Dark Brown in 3" (7.5 cm) lengths. Add fringe to end of rows on Tail ***(Figs. 7a & b, page 41)***. Trim evenly.

Fold Tail in half lengthwise, matching **wrong** side of sc on Row 3 and **wrong** side of free loops. Sew seam; then sew Tail to Body.

FINISHING

Cut a 12" (30.5 cm) length of Main Color yarn. Thread yarn needle and sew Rnds 14-17 of Head securely across Rnds 7-10 of Body.

With Dark Brown and using straight stitch ***(Fig. 13, page 42)***, add two x's on each side of snout for nostrils.

HAIR (fringe)

With Brown, cut strands in the following lengths:

116 Strands 3" (7.5 cm) long
250 Strands 4" (10 cm) long
80 Strands 6" (15 cm) long

Adding Body Hair

Note: To add Hair to Body, hold Body upside down and add fringe. This will make the Hair lay flat when Body is right side up.

- Add 9 strands of 3" (7.5 cm) fringe around each exposed free loop on Rnd 3 of each Leg ***(Figs. 7c & d, page 41)***. Do **not** add fringe in 3 free loops under Belly.
- Add 80 strands of 3" (7.5 cm) fringe around each exposed free loop created when working Rnd 2 of Body.
- Add 80 strands of 4" (10 cm) fringe around each exposed free loop created when working Rnd 6 of Body.
- Add 56 strands of 4" (10 cm) fringe around each exposed free loop created when working Rnd 11 of Body.
- Add 36 strands of 6" (15 cm) fringe around each exposed free loop on Rnd 16 (exposed loops on the seam).
- Add 18 strands of 6" (15 cm) fringe along center seam to cover seam.

Note: When sewing the Head onto the Body, it may have covered some of the exposed loops on Rnd 16. Use stitch posts to add fringe around Head.

Adding Head Hair

Use stitch posts to add fringe ***(Figs. 7e & f, page 41)***.

- Add 4 strands of 6" (15 cm) fringe in front of each Horn down to Ear.
- Add 4 strands of 6" (15 cm) fringe in back of each Horn down to Ear.
- Add 4 strands of 4" (10 cm) fringe in front and back of each Ear beside the 6" (15 cm) strands.
- Add 10 strands of 6" (15 cm) fringe across top of Head.
- Working back and forth over the top and back of Head, add the remaining 4" (10 cm) strands to fill Head with hair.

Trim hair around eyes if desired.

TAN HIGHLAND COW

INTERMEDIATE

Finished Measurements

Length: 9" (23 cm)

Height: 8" (20.5 cm)

SHOPPING LIST

Yarn (Medium Weight) [MEDIUM 4]

[3.5 ounces, 185 yards (100 grams, 170 meters) per skein]:

- ☐ Main Color (Tan) - 1 skein
- ☐ Dark Brown - 1 skein **or** 23 yards (21 meters)
- ☐ Cream - 1 skein **or** 25 yards (23 meters)

Crochet Hook

- ☐ Size G (4 mm) **or** size needed for gauge

Additional Supplies

- ☐ 12 mm Safety eyes - 2
- ☐ Polyester fiberfill
- ☐ Yarn needle

For Tan Highland Cow, work same as Highland Cow, pages 3-8, using Tan as the Main Color.

HAIR (fringe)

With Main Color, cut strands in the following lengths:

116 Strands 3" (7.5 cm) long
250 Strands 4" (10 cm) long
92 Strands 6" (15 cm) long

With Cream, cut strands in the following lengths:

6 Strands 4" (10 cm) long
6 Strands 6" (15 cm) long

Adding Body Hair

Note: Use Tan strands unless otherwise indicated. To add Hair to Body, hold Body upside down and add fringe. This will make the Hair lay flat when Body is right side up.

- Add 9 strands of 3" (7.5 cm) fringe around each exposed free loop on Rnd 3 of each Leg ***(Figs. 7c & d, page 41)***. Do **not** add fringe in 3 free loops under Belly.
- Add 80 strands of 3" (7.5 cm) fringe around each exposed free loop created when working Rnd 2 of Body.
- Add 80 strands of 4" (10 cm) fringe around each exposed free loop created when working Rnd 6 of Body.
- Add 56 strands of 4" (10 cm) fringe around each exposed free loop created when working Rnd 11 of Body.
- Add 36 strands of 6" (15 cm) fringe around each exposed free loop on Rnd 16 (exposed loops on the seam).
- Add 18 strands of 6" (15 cm) fringe along center seam to cover seam.
- Add strands of 6" (15 cm) fringe under head in chest, using 12 strands of Tan and 6 strands of Cream, placing Cream strands where desired.

Note: When sewing the Head onto the Body, it may have covered some of the exposed loops on Rnd 16. Use stitch posts to add fringe around Head.

Adding Head Hair

Note: Use Main Color strands unless otherwise indicated. Use stitch posts to add fringe ***(Figs. 7e & f, page 41)***.

- Add 4 strands of 6" (15 cm) fringe in front of each Horn down to Ear.
- Add 4 strands of 6" (15 cm) fringe in back of each Horn down to Ear.
- Add 4 strands of 4" (10 cm) fringe in front and back of each Ear beside the 6" (15 cm) strands.
- Add 10 strands of 6" (15 cm) fringe across top of Head.
- Working back and forth over the top and back of Head, add the remaining 4" (10 cm) Main Color and 4" (10 cm) Cream strands to fill Head with hair.

Trim hair around eyes if desired.

BLANKET

INTERMEDIATE

Finished Size

30½" wide x 37¾" long

(77.5 cm x 96 cm)

SHOPPING LIST

Yarn (Medium Weight) 

[3.5 ounces, 185 yards (100 grams, 170 meters) per skein]:

- ☐ Taupe - 6 skeins
- ☐ Gold - 4 skeins
- ☐ Tan - 2 skeins
- ☐ Brown - 2 skeins
- ☐ Dark Brown - 1 skein **or** 70 yards (64 meters)
- ☐ Cream - 1 skein **or** 85 yards (77.5 meters)
- ☐ Pink - 1 skein **or** 40 yards (36.5 meters)

Crochet Hooks

- ☐ Sizes G (4 mm) **and** H (5 mm) **or** sizes needed for gauge

Additional Supplies

- ☐ 10mm Safety eyes - 20
- ☐ Polyester fiberfill
- ☐ Yarn needle
- ☐ Removable stitch markers (optional)

GAUGE INFORMATION

With smaller size hook,
16 sts and 18 rows = 4" (10 cm)
With larger size hook,
15 sts and 14 rows/rnds = 4" (10 cm)
One Motif = 7¼" (18.5 cm)
Gauge Swatch: 7¼" (18.5 cm) wide
Work one Motif, page 14, including Trim.
Save time, check your gauge.

STITCH GUIDE

SINGLE CROCHET 2 TOGETHER ***(abbreviated sc2tog)***

Pull up a loop in each of next 2 sts, YO and draw through all 3 loops on hook ***(Fig. A)*** **(counts as one sc)**.

Fig. A

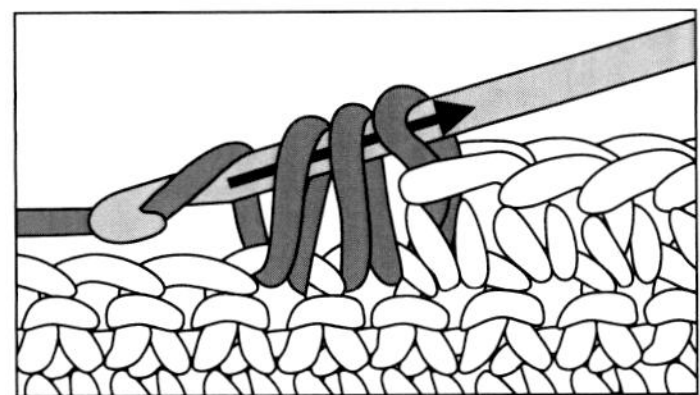

SINGLE CROCHET 3 TOGETHER ***(abbreviated sc3tog)***

Pull up a loop in each of next 3 sts, YO and draw through all 3 loops on hook ***(Fig. B)*** **(counts as one sc)**.

Fig. B

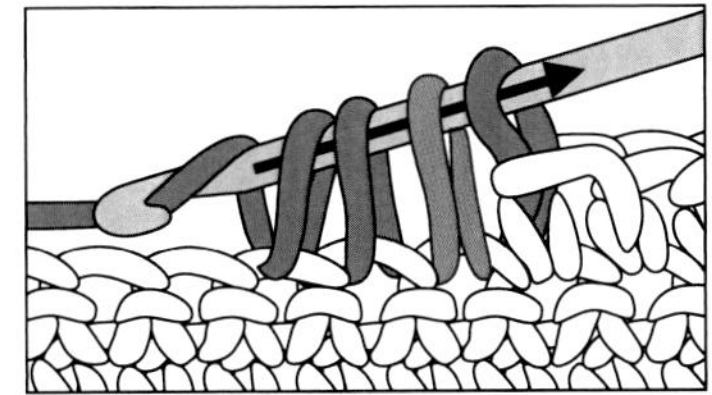

FRONT POST SINGLE CROCHET ***(abbreviated FPsc)***

Insert hook from **front** to **back** around post of st indicated ***(Fig. C)***, YO and pull up a loop, YO and draw through both loops on hook. Skip st **behind** FPsc.

Fig. C

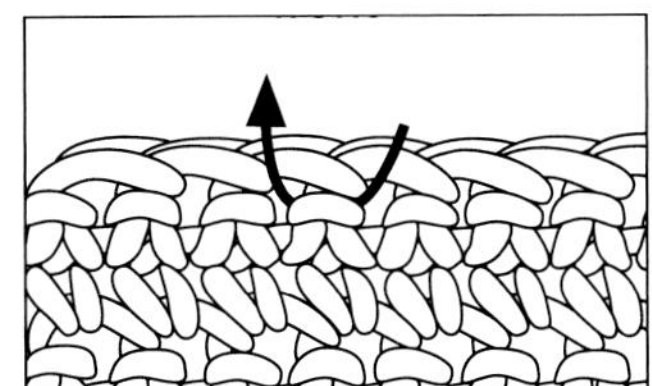

BEGINNING STAR STITCH

Insert hook in middle horizontal bar of last hdc made, YO and pull up a loop, insert hook in bottom leg of hdc, YO and pull up a loop, insert hook in same stitch as hdc, YO and pull up a loop, (insert hook in **next** st, YO and pull up a loop) twice, YO and draw through all 6 loops on hook ***(Fig. D)***, ch 1 (to form eyelet).

Fig. D

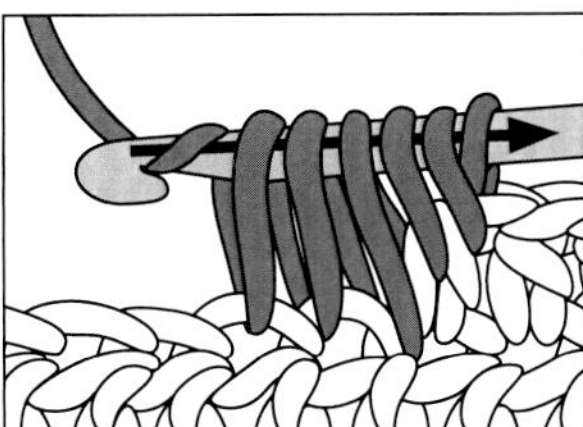

STAR STITCH

Insert hook in eyelet of last Star Stitch made, YO and pull up a loop, insert hook in bottom leg of Star Stitch, YO and pull up a loop, insert hook in base stitch of Star Stitch, YO and pull up a loop, (insert hook in **next** st, YO and pull up a loop) twice, YO, draw through all 6 loops on hook ***(Fig. E)***, ch 1 (to form eyelet).

Fig. E

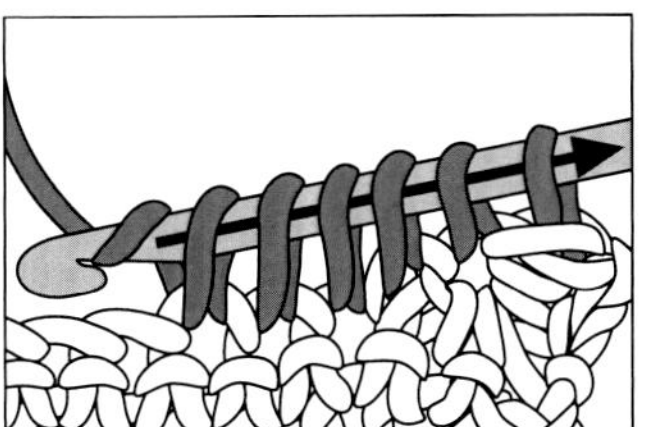

MOTIF (Make 20)

With larger size hook and Taupe, ch 23.

Row 1: Sc in second ch from hook, dc in next ch, (sc in next ch, dc in next ch) across: 22 sts.

Row 2 (Right side)**:** Ch 1, turn; sc in each st across.

Note: Mark Row 2 as **right** side **and** bottom edge.

Row 3: Ch 3 **(counts as first dc)**, turn; sc in next sc, (dc in next sc, sc in next sc) across.

Row 4: Ch 1, turn; sc in each st across.

Row 5: Ch 1, turn; sc in first sc, dc in next sc, (sc in next sc, dc in next sc) across.

Row 6: Ch 1, turn; sc in each st across.

Rows 7-22: Repeat Rows 3-6, 4 times.

Edging: Ch 1, do **not** turn, 2 sc in last sc made; working in end of rows, work 20 sc evenly spaced across to beginning ch; working in free loops of beginning ch ***(Fig. 5b, page 40)***, 3 sc in ch at base of first sc on Row 1, sc in next 20 chs, 3 sc in last ch; working in end of rows, work 20 sc evenly spaced across to Row 22; 3 sc in first sc, sc in next 20 sc and in same st as first sc; join with slip st to first sc, finish off: 92 sc.

TRIM

Rnd 1: With **right** side facing and using larger size hook, join Gold with slip st in center sc of any corner 3-sc group, ch 2 (does **not** count as a st); 3 hdc in same st as slip st, ★ † work Beginning Star St, work Star Sts across to center sc of next corner 3-sc group †, 3 hdc in center sc; repeat from ★ 2 times **more**, then repeat from † to † once; join with slip st to first hdc: 12 hdc and 44 ch-1 sps.

Rnd 2: Slip st in next hdc, ch 2 (does **not** count as a st); 3 hdc in same st as slip st, hdc in next hdc, ★ † 2 hdc in each ch-1 sp (eyelet) across to next corner 3-hdc group †, hdc in next hdc, 3 hdc in center hdc, hdc in next hdc; repeat from ★ 2 times **more**, then repeat from † to † once, hdc in next st; join with slip st to first hdc, finish off: 108 hdc.

COW APPLIQUÉ

(Make 20 TOTAL)

(Make 10 Cows with a Brown Head, Body & Ears **and** 10 Cows with a Tan Head, Body & Ears)

HEAD

Rnd 1 (Right side)**:** With smaller size hook and Pink, ch 4; 2 sc in second ch from hook, sc in next ch, 4 sc in last ch; working in free loops on opposite side of ch, sc in next ch, 2 sc in next ch; join with slip st to first sc: 10 sc.

Note: Mark Rnd 1 as **right** side.

Rnd 2: Ch 1, 2 sc in same st as joining, sc in next 3 sc, 2 sc in each of next 2 sc, sc in next 3 sc, 2 sc in last sc; join with slip st to first sc, finish off: 14 sc.

Rnd 3: With **right** side facing and using smaller size hook, join Cream with slip st in same st as joining; ch 1, 2 sc in same st, sc in next 5 sc, 2 sc in next 2 sc, sc in next 5 sc, 2 sc in last sc; join with slip st to first sc, finish off: 18 sc.

Row 4: With **right** side facing and using smaller size hook, join Main Color (Brown or Tan) with slip st in same st as joining; ch 1, work FPsc around each of next 9 sc, leave remaining sts unworked: 9 FPsc.

Row 5: Ch 1, turn; 2 sc in first FPsc, sc in next 7 FPsc, 2 sc in last FPsc: 11 sc.

Row 6: Ch 1, turn; 2 sc in first sc, sc in next 9 sc, 2 sc in last sc: 13 sc.

Rows 7-9: Ch 1, turn; sc in first sc and in each sc across.

Insert safety eyes between Rnds 6 and 7, placing eyes 4 stitches apart ***(see Attaching Safety Eyes, page 40)***.

Row 10: Ch 1, turn; beginning in first sc, sc2tog, sc in next 9 sc, sc2tog: 11 sc.

Row 11: Ch 1, turn; beginning in first sc, sc3tog, sc in next 5 sc, sc3tog: 7 sc.

Edging: Ch 1, turn; beginning in first sc, sc2tog, sc in next 3 sc, sc2tog; work 8 sc evenly spaced across to muzzle; sc in Back Loop Only of next 9 sc ***(Fig. 4, page 40)***; work 8 sc evenly spaced across; join with slip st to first sc, finish off leaving a 12" (30.5 cm) length for sewing.

BODY

Row 1 (Right side)**:** With smaller size hook and Main Color (Brown or Tan), ch 10; 2 sc in second ch from hook, sc in next 7 chs, 2 sc in last ch: 11 sc.

Note: Mark Row 1 as **right** side.

Rows 2-6: Ch 1, turn; sc in each sc across.

Do **not** finish off.

FIRST LEG

Row 1: Ch 1, turn; sc in first 4 sc, leave remaining 7 sc unworked.

Rows 2 and 3: Ch 1, turn; sc in each sc across.

Finish off.

Row 4 (Hoof)**:** With **wrong** side facing and using smaller size hook, join Dark Brown with slip st in first sc of First Leg; ch 1, sc in same st and in last 3 sc.

Row 5: Ch 1, turn; beginning in first sc, sc2tog twice; finish off leaving an 8" (20.5 cm) length for sewing: 2 sc.

SECOND LEG

Row 1: With **right** side facing and using smaller size hook, skip next 3 unworked sc from First Leg and join Main Color (Brown or Tan) with slip st in next sc; ch 1, sc in same st and in last 3 sc: 4 sc.

Rows 2 and 3: Ch 1, turn; sc in each sc across.

Finish off.

Row 4 (Hoof)**:** With **wrong** side facing and using smaller size hook, join Dark Brown with slip st in first sc of Second Leg; ch 1, sc in same st and in last 3 sc.

Row 5: Ch 1, turn; beginning in first sc, sc2tog twice; finish off leaving an 8" (20.5 cm) length for sewing: 2 sc.

HORN (Make 2)

Row 1 (Right side)**:** With smaller size hook and Cream, ch 10; working in back ridge of chs ***(Fig. 3, page 40)***, slip st in second ch from hook and in next 2 chs, hdc in next 3 chs, dc in last 3 chs; finish off leaving a 10" (25.5 cm) length for sewing.

Note: Mark Row 1 as **right** side.

EAR (Make 2)

Rnd 1 (Right side)**:** With smaller size hook and Main Color (Brown or Tan), ch 4; 9 dc in fourth ch from hook **(3 skipped chs count as one dc)**; join with slip st to first dc; finish off leaving an 8" (20.5 cm) length for sewing: 10 dc.

Note: Mark Rnd 1 as **right** side.

COW ASSEMBLY

Using photo as a guide for placement, having **wrong** side of Appliqué pieces against **right** side of Motif and using long ends:

- With matching Main Color (Brown or Tan), sew Body to Motif, having bottom of Hooves above Row 2.
- Sew Hooves in place.
- With Dark Brown and using straight stitch ***(Fig. 13, page 42)***, add two x's on each side of muzzle for nostrils.
- Place Head over top row or two of Body and sew to Motif, stuffing with polyester fiberfill before closing.
- For Collar, turn Motif upside down with the **right** side facing. With smaller size hook and Dark Brown, work surface slip sts at the edge of Row 4 of Head ***(see Surface Slip Stitches, page 40)***, beginning and ending around muzzle, where the muzzle overlaps the Body; finish off.
- Thread yarn needle with a 10" (25.5 cm) length of Gold and satin stitch Bell on Body ***(Fig. 14, page 42)***, centered below the muzzle and collar.
- Sew Horns to Head and Motif.
- Sew Ears below the point where Horn meets the Head.
- Cut 400, 3" (7.5 cm) length of Brown (40 strands for **each** Brown Cow).

- Cut 200, 3" (7.5 cm) lengths of Tan and 200, 3" (7.5 cm) length of Cream (20 strands of **each** color for **each** Tan Cow).
  Note: To add Hair to Head, hold Front Panel upside down and add fringe. This will make the Hair lay flat when Body is right side up. Use stitch posts to add fringe ***(Figs. 7e & f, page 41)***.
- Add 4 strands of fringe in from Ear down the side of Head on each side.
- Working across Row 10, add fringe across and down each side of Head. Fill in top of Head with fringe.

MOTIF ASSEMBLY

With **wrong** sides together, matching sts at bottom edge of Tan Cow Motif with sts at top edge of Brown Cow Motif, whipstitch Motifs together with Gold ***(Fig. 6, page 40)***, working through **both** loops of **both** pieces and beginning and ending in center hdc of each corner.

Continue in same manner, joining 5 Motifs into 4 vertical strips, alternating the Main Color of the Cows throughout.
Join strips in same manner.

EDGING

Rnd 1: With **right** side facing, join Gold with slip st in center hdc of any corner 3-hdc group; ch 2 (does **not** count as a st); 3 hdc in same st as slip st, ★ † work Beginning Star St, work Star Sts across to center sc of next corner 3-sc group using the Motif joining as a st †, 3 hdc in center sc; repeat from ★ 2 times **more**, then repeat from † to † once; join with slip st to first hdc.

Rnd 2: Slip st in next hdc, ch 2 (does **not** count as a st); 3 hdc in same st as slip st, hdc in next hdc, ★ † 2 hdc in each ch-1 sp (eyelet) across to next corner 3-hdc group †, hdc in next hdc, 3 hdc in center hdc, hdc in next hdc; repeat from ★ 2 times **more**, then repeat from † to † once, hdc in next st; join with slip st to first hdc, finish off.

Is your pasture too full?

If you prefer not to have as many cows on your afghan, feel free to do you own thing!

The following yarn amounts are for one cow **ONLY**:

Main Color – 17 yards (15.5 meters)
Cream – 5 yards (4.6 meters)
Dark Brown – 4 yards (3.7 meters)
Pink – 2 yards (1.8 meters)
Gold – 12" (30.5 mm)

PILLOW

INTERMEDIATE

Finished Size

16" (40.5 cm) square

SHOPPING LIST

Yarn (Medium Weight) 

[3.5 ounces, 185 yards
(100 grams, 170 meters) per skein]:

- ☐ Taupe - 3 skeins
- ☐ Gold - 2 skeins
- ☐ Tan - 45 yards (41 meters)
- ☐ Brown - 45 yards (41 meters)
- ☐ Dark Brown - 20 yards (18.5 meters)
- ☐ Cream - 25 yards (23 meters)
- ☐ Pink - 10 yards (9 meters)

Crochet Hooks

- ☐ Sizes G (4 mm) **and** H (5 mm) **or** sizes needed for gauge

Additional Supplies

- ☐ 10mm Safety eyes - 8
- ☐ 16" (40.5 cm) square Pillow insert
- ☐ Polyester fiberfill
- ☐ Yarn needle
- ☐ Removable stitch markers (optional)

GAUGE INFORMATION

With smaller size hook,
16 sts and 18 rows = 4" (10 cm)
With larger size hook,
15 sts and 14 rows/rnds = 4" (10 cm)
One Motif = 7¼" (18.5 cm) wide
Gauge Swatch: 7¼" (18.5 cm) wide
Work one Motif, page 24.
Save time, check your gauge.

STITCH GUIDE

SINGLE CROCHET 2 TOGETHER
(abbreviated sc2tog)

Pull up a loop in each of next 2 sts, YO and draw through all 3 loops on hook ***(Fig. A)*** **(counts as one sc)**.

Fig. A

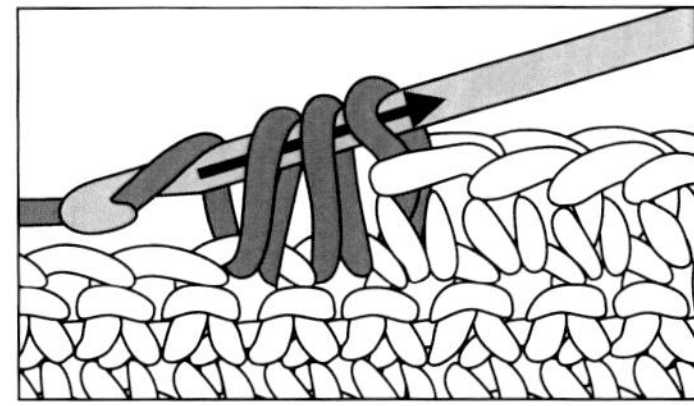

SINGLE CROCHET 3 TOGETHER
(abbreviated sc3tog)

Pull up a loop in each of next 3 sts, YO and draw through all 3 loops on hook ***(Fig. B)*** **(counts as one sc)**.

Fig. B

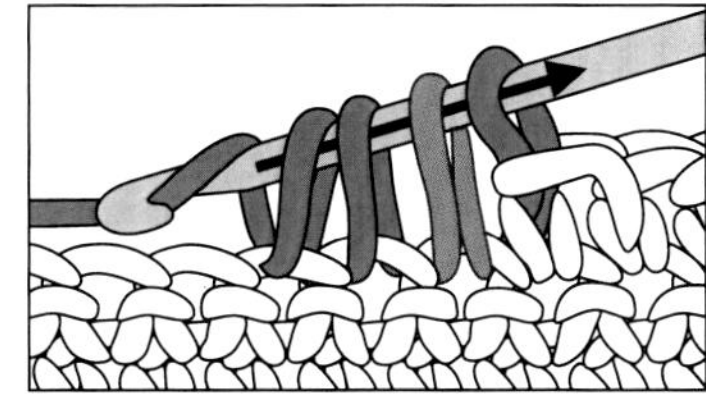

FRONT POST SINGLE CROCHET
(abbreviated FPsc)

Insert hook from **front** to **back** around post of st indicated ***(Fig. C)***, YO and pull up a loop, YO and draw through both loops on hook. Skip st **behind** FPsc.

Fig. C

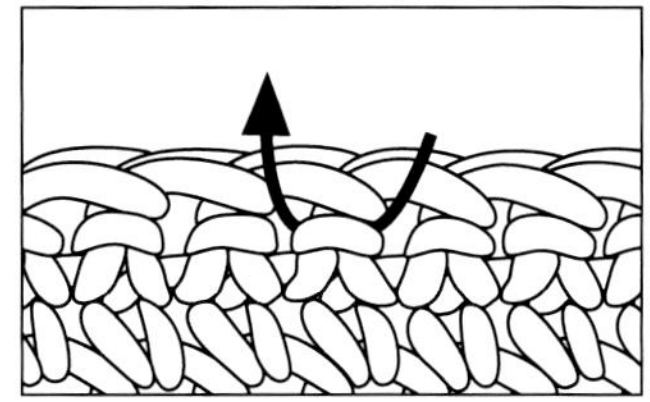

BEGINNING STAR STITCH

Insert hook in middle horizontal bar of last hdc made, YO and pull up a loop, insert hook in bottom leg of hdc, YO and pull up a loop, insert hook in same stitch as hdc, YO and pull up a loop, (insert hook in **next** st, YO and pull up a loop) twice, YO and draw through all 6 loops ***(Fig. D)***, ch 1 (to form eyelet).

Fig. D

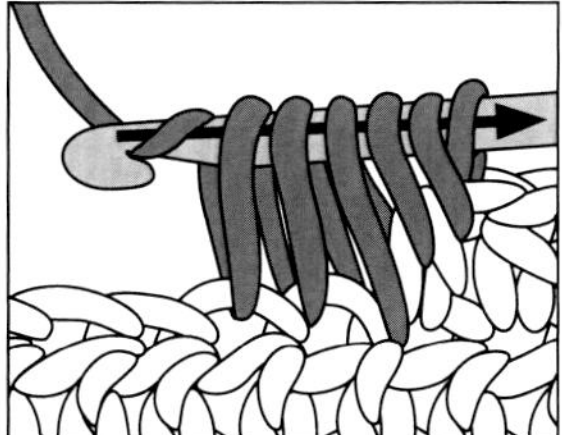

STAR STITCH

Insert hook in eyelet of last Star Stitch made, YO and pull up a loop, insert hook in bottom leg of Star Stitch, YO and pull up a loop, insert hook in base stitch of Star Stitch, YO and pull up a loop, (insert hook in **next** st, YO and pull up a loop) twice, YO, draw through all 6 loops ***(Fig. E)***, ch 1 (to form eyelet).

Fig. E

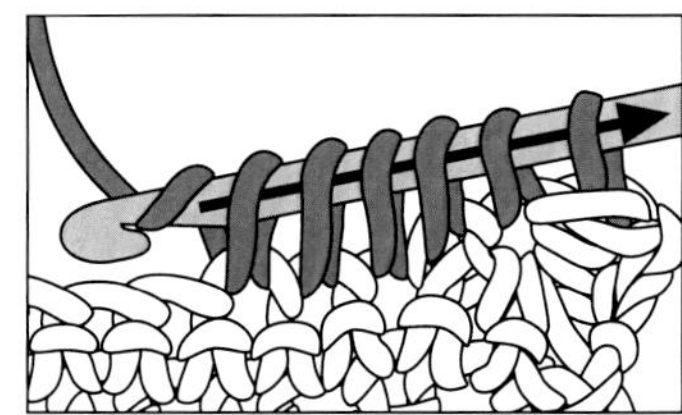

PATTERN NOTES

Pillow is made in sections: 4 Motifs for the Front, and Cow Appliqué components (Body & Legs, Head, Horns, and Ears) and the Back. Hair will be added like fringe.

FRONT MOTIF (Make 4)

With larger size hook and Taupe, ch 23.

Row 1: Sc in second ch from hook, dc in next ch, (sc in next ch, dc in next ch) across: 22 sts.

Row 2 (Right side)**:** Ch 1, turn; sc in each st across.

Note: Loop a short piece of yarn around any stitch to mark Row 2 as **right** side **and** bottom edge.

Row 3: Ch 3 **(counts as first dc)**, turn; sc in next sc, (dc in next sc, sc in next sc) across.

Row 4: Ch 1, turn; sc in each st across.

Row 5: Ch 1, turn; sc in first sc, dc in next sc, (sc in next sc, dc in next sc) across.

Row 6: Ch 1, turn; sc in each st across.

Rows 7-22: Repeat Rows 3-6, 4 times.

Edging: Ch 1, do **not** turn, 2 sc in last sc made; working in end of rows, work 20 sc evenly spaced across to beginning ch; working in free loops of beginning ch *(**Fig. 5b, page 40**)*, 3 sc in ch at base of first sc on Row 1, sc in next 20 chs, 3 sc in last ch; working in end of rows, work 20 sc evenly spaced across to Row 22; 3 sc in first sc on Row 22, sc in next 20 sc and in same st as first sc; join with slip st to first sc, finish off: 92 sc.

TRIM

Rnd 1: With **right** side facing and using larger size hook, join Gold with slip st in center sc of any corner 3-sc group, ch 2 (does **not** count as a st); 3 hdc in same st as slip st, ★ † work Beginning Star St, work Star Sts across to center sc of next corner 3-sc group †, 3 hdc in center sc; repeat from ★ 2 times **more**, then repeat from † to † once; join with slip st to first hdc: 12 hdc and 44 ch-1 sps.

Rnd 2: Slip st in next hdc, ch 2 (does **not** count as a st); 3 hdc in same st as slip st, hdc in next hdc, ★ † 2 hdc in each ch-1 sp (eyelet) across to next corner 3-hdc group †, hdc in next hdc, 3 hdc in center hdc, hdc in next hdc; repeat from ★ 2 times **more**, then repeat from † to † once, hdc in next st; join with slip st to first hdc, finish off: 108 hdc.

COW APPLIQUÉ

(Make 4 total)

(Make 2 Cows with a Brown Head, Body & Ears and 2 Cows with a Tan Head, Body & Ears)

HEAD

Rnd 1 (Right side)**:** With smaller size hook and Pink, ch 4; 2 sc in second ch from hook, sc in next ch, 4 sc in last ch; working in free loops on opposite side of ch, sc in next ch, 2 sc in next ch; join with slip st to first sc: 10 sc.

Note: Mark Rnd 1 as **right** side.

Rnd 2: Ch 1, 2 sc in same st as joining, sc in next 3 sc, 2 sc in each of next 2 sc, sc in next 3 sc, 2 sc in last sc; join with slip st to first sc, finish off: 14 sc.

Rnd 3: With **right** side facing, join Cream with slip st in first same st as joining; ch 1, 2 sc in same st, sc in next 5 sc, 2 sc in next 2 sc, sc in next 5 sc, 2 sc in last sc; join with slip st to first sc, finish off: 18 sc.

Row 4: With **right** side facing, join Main Color (Brown or Tan) with slip st in same st as joining; ch 1, work FPsc around each of next 9 sc, leaving remaining sts unworked: 9 FPsc.

Row 5: Ch 1, turn; 2 sc in first FPsc, sc in next 7 FPsc, 2 sc in last FPsc: 11 sc.

Row 6: Ch 1, turn; 2 sc in first sc, sc in next 9 sc, 2 sc in last sc: 13 sc.

Rows 7-9: Ch 1, turn; sc in first sc and in each sc across.

Insert safety eyes between Rnds 6 and 7, placing eyes 4 stitches apart ***(see Attaching Safety Eyes, page 40)***.

Row 10: Ch 1, turn; beginning in first sc, sc2tog, sc in next 9 sc, sc2tog: 11 sc.

Row 11: Ch 1, turn; beginning in first sc, sc3tog, sc in next 5 sc, sc3tog: 7 sc.

Edging: Ch 1, turn; beginning in first sc, sc2tog, sc in next 3 sc, sc2tog; work 8 sc evenly spaced across to muzzle; sc in Back Loop Only of next 9 sc ***(Fig. 4, page 40)***; work 8 sc evenly spaced across; join with slip st to first sc, finish off leaving a 12" (30.5 cm) length for sewing.

BODY

Row 1 (Right side)**:** With smaller size hook and Main Color (Brown or Tan), ch 10; 2 sc in second ch from hook, sc in next 7 chs, 2 sc in last ch: 11 sc.

Note: Mark Row 1 as **right** side.

Rows 2-6: Ch 1, turn; sc in each sc across.

Do **not** finish off.

FIRST LEG

Row 1: Ch 1, turn; sc in first 4 sc, leave remaining 7 sc unworked.

Rows 2 and 3: Ch 1, turn; sc in each sc across.

Finish off.

Row 4: With **wrong** side facing, join Dark Brown with slip st in first sc of First Leg; ch 1, sc in same st and in last 3 sc.

Row 5: Ch 1, turn; beginning in first sc, sc2tog twice, finish off leaving an 8" (20.5 cm) length for sewing: 2 sc.

SECOND LEG

Row 1: With **right** side facing, skip next 3 unworked sc from First Leg and join Main Color (Brown or Tan) with slip st in next sc; ch 1, sc in same st and in last 3 sc: 4 sc.

Rows 2 and 3: Ch 1, turn; sc in each sc across.

Finish off.

Row 4 (Hoof)**:** With **wrong** side facing, join Dark Brown with slip st in first sc of Second Leg; ch 1, sc in same st and in last 3 sc.

Row 5: Ch 1, turn; beginning in first sc, sc2tog twice, finish off leaving an 8" (20.5 cm) length for sewing: 2 sc.

HORN (Make 2)

Row 1 (Right side)**:** With smaller size hook and Cream, ch 10; working in back ridge of chs ***(Fig. 3, page 40)***, slip st in second ch from hook and in next 2 chs, hdc in next 3 chs, dc in last 3 chs; finish off leaving a 10" (25.5 cm) length for sewing.

Note: Mark Row 1 as **right** side.

EAR (Make 2)

Rnd 1 (Right side)**:** With smaller size hook and Main Color (Brown or Tan), ch 4, 9 dc in fourth ch from hook **(3 skipped chs count as one dc)**; join with slip st to first dc, finish off leaving an 8" (20.5 cm) length for sewing: 10 dc.

Note: Mark Rnd 1 as **right** side.

COW ASSEMBLY

Using photo as a guide for placement, having **wrong** side of Appliqué pieces against **right** side of Motif and using long ends:

- With matching Main Color (Brown or Tan), sew Body to Motif, having bottom of Hooves above Row 2.
- Sew Hooves in place.
- With Dark Brown and using straight stitch ***(Fig. 13, page 42)***, add two x's on each side of muzzle for nostrils.
- Place Head over top row or two of Body and sew to Motif, stuffing with polyester fiberfill before closing.
- For Collar, turn Motif upside down with the **right** side facing. With smaller size hook and Dark Brown, work surface slip sts at the edge of Row 4 of Head ***(see Surface Slip Stitches, page 40)***, beginning and ending around muzzle, where the muzzle overlaps the Body; finish off.
- Thread yarn needle with a 10" (25.5 cm) length of Gold and satin stitch Bell on Body ***(Fig. 14, page 42)***, centered below the muzzle and collar.
- Sew Horns to Head and Motif.
- Sew Ears below the point where Horn meets the Head.
- Cut 80, 3" (7.5 cm) lengths of Brown (40 strands for each Brown Cow).
- Cut 40, 3" (7.5 cm) lengths of Tan and 40, 3" (7.5 cm) length of Cream (20 strands of each color for each Tan Cow).

Note: To add Hair to Head, hold Front Panel upside down and add fringe. This will make the Hair lay flat when Body is right side up. Use stitch posts to add fringe ***(Figs. 7e & f, page 41)***.

- Add 4 strands of fringe in from Ear down the side of Head on each side.
- Working across Row 10, add fringe across and down each side of Head. Fill in top of Head with fringe.

MOTIF ASSEMBLY

With **wrong** sides together, matching sts at bottom edge of Tan Cow Motif with sts at top edge of Brown Cow Motif, whipstitch Motifs together with Gold ***(Fig. 6, page 40)***, working through **both** loops of **both** pieces and beginning and ending in center hdc of each corner.

With **wrong** sides together, matching sts at bottom edge of remaining Brown Cow Motif with sts at top edge of remaining Tan Cow Motif, whipstitch Motifs together in same manner.

With **wrong** sides of both Strips together and having bottom edges at the same edge, whipstitch Strips together in same manner.

FRONT EDGING

Rnd 1: With **right** side facing, join Gold with slip st in center hdc of any corner 3-hdc group; ch 2 (does **not** count as a st); 3 hdc in same st as slip st, ★ † work Beginning Star St, work Star Sts across to center sc of next corner 3-sc group using the Motif joining as a st †, 3 hdc in center sc; repeat from ★ 2 times **more**, then repeat from † to † once; join with slip st to first hdc: 12 hdc and 108 ch-1 sps.

Rnd 2: Slip st in next hdc, ch 2 (does **not** count as a st); 3 hdc in same st as slip st, hdc in next hdc, ★ † 2 hdc in each ch-1 sp (eyelet) across to next corner 3-hdc group †, hdc in next hdc, 3 hdc in center hdc, hdc in next hdc; repeat from ★ 2 times **more**, then repeat from † to † once, hdc in next st; join with slip st to first hdc, finish off: 228 hdc.

BACK

With larger size hook and Taupe, ch 53.

Row 1: Sc in second ch from hook, dc in next ch, (sc in next ch, dc in next ch) across: 52 sts.

Row 2 (Right side)**:** Ch 1, turn; sc in each st across.

Note: Mark Row 2 as **right** side.

Row 3: Ch 3 **(counts as first dc)**, turn; sc in next sc, (dc in next sc, sc in next sc) across.

Row 4: Ch 1, turn; sc in each st across.

Row 5: Ch 1, turn; sc in first sc, dc in next sc, (sc in next sc, dc in next sc) across.

Row 6: Ch 1, turn; sc in each st across.

Rows 7-50: Repeat Rows 3-6, 11 times.

Edging: Ch 1, do **not** turn, 2 sc in last sc made; working in end of rows, work 50 sc evenly spaced across to beginning ch; working in free loops of beginning ch, 3 sc in ch at base of first sc on Row 1, sc in next 50 chs, 3 sc in last ch; working in end of rows, work 50 sc evenly spaced across to Row 50; 3 sc in first sc on Row 50, sc in next 50 sc and in same sc as first sc; join with slip st to first sc, finish off: 212 sc.

TRIM

Rnd 1: With **right** side facing and using larger size hook, join Gold with slip st in center sc of any corner 3-sc group, ch 2 (does **not** count as a st); 3 hdc in same st as slip st, ★ † work Beginning Star St, work Star Sts across to center sc of next corner 3-sc group †, 3 hdc in center sc; repeat from ★ 2 times **more**, then repeat from † to † once; join with slip st to first hdc: 12 hdc and 104 ch-1 sps.

Rnd 2: Slip st in next hdc, ch 2 (does **not** count as a st); 3 hdc in same st as slip st, hdc in next st, ★ † 2 hdc in each ch-1 sp (eyelet) across to next corner 3-hdc group †, hdc in next hdc, 3 hdc in center hdc, hdc in next hdc; repeat from ★ 2 times **more**, then repeat from † to † once, hdc in next st; join with slip st to first hdc, finish off: 228 hdc.

FINISHING

With **wrong** sides of Front and Back together, Front facing you and working through **inside** loops on **both** pieces, join Gold with slip st in any corner hdc; slip st through inside loops around, inserting pillow insert before closing; join with slip st to first st, finish off.

HIGHLAND COW PUDGIE

EASY

Finished Height: 4" (10 cm)

SHOPPING LIST

Yarn (Medium Weight) MEDIUM 4

[3.5 ounces, 185 yards (100 grams, 170 meters) per skein]:

- ☐ Brown - 1 skein
- ☐ Cream - 1 skein **or** 8 yards (7.5 meters)
- ☐ Black - 2 yards (1.8 meters)

Crochet Hook

- ☐ Size G (4 mm) **or** size needed for gauge

Additional Supplies

- ☐ Polyester fiberfill
- ☐ Yarn needle

GAUGE INFORMATION

8 sc and 9 rows/rnds = 2" (5 cm)

Gauge Swatch: 2" (5 cm) diameter

Work same as Head & Body through Rnd 4: 32 sc.

Save time, check your gauge.

HEAD & BODY

Rnd 1 (Right side)**:** With Brown and beginning at bottom of Body, make an adjustable ring, work 8 sc in ring ***(Figs. 2a-d, page 39)***; do **not** join, place marker to indicate the beginning of the round ***(Fig. 1, page 39)***.

Note: Loop a short piece of yarn around any stitch to mark Rnd 1 as **right** side.

Rnd 2: 2 Sc in each sc around: 16 sc.

Rnd 3: (Sc in next sc, 2 sc in next sc) around: 24 sc.

Rnd 4: (Sc in next 2 sc, 2 sc in next sc) around: 32 sc.

Rnd 5: (Sc in next 3 sc, 2 sc in next sc) around: 40 sc.

Rnds 6 and 7: Sc in each sc around.

Rnd 8: (Sc in next 3 sc, sc2tog) around: 32 sc.

Rnds 9 and 10: Sc in each sc around.

Rnd 11: (Sc in next 2 sc, sc2tog) around: 24 sc.

Rnds 12-15: Sc in each sc around.

Rnd 16: (Sc in next sc, sc2tog) around: 16 sc.

Rnd 17-19: Sc in each sc around.

Stuff piece with polyester fiberfill.

Rnd 20: Sc2tog around; slip st in next sc, finish off leaving an 8" (20.5 cm) length for sewing: 8 sts.

Thread yarn needle with end and weave yarn through Front Loop Only of remaining st to close ***(Fig. 4, page 40)***; secure end.

SNOUT

Rnd 1 (Right side)**:** With Cream, ch 4; 2 sc in second ch from hook, sc in next ch, 4 sc in last ch; working in free loops on opposite side of ch ***(Fig. 5b, page 40)***, sc in next ch, 2 sc in next ch; join with slip st to first sc: 10 sc.

Note: Mark Rnd 1 as **right** side.

Rnd 2: Ch 1, 2 sc in same st as joining, sc in next 3 sc, 2 sc in each of next 2 sc, sc in next 3 sc, 2 sc in last sc; join with slip to first sc, finish off leaving an 8" (20.5 cm) length for sewing.

HORN (Make 2)

Rnd 1 (Right side)**:** With Cream, ch 2, 3 sc in second ch from hook; do **not** join, place marker to indicate the beginning of the round.

Note: Mark Rnd 1 as **right** side.

Rnd 2: 2 Sc in next sc, sc in next 2 sc: 4 sc.

Rnd 3: 2 Sc in next sc, sc in next 3 sc: 5 sc.

Rnd 4: 2 Sc in next sc, sc in next 4 sc: 6 sc.

Rnd 5: 2 Sc in next sc, sc in next 5 sc: 7 sc.

Rnd 6: 2 Sc in next sc, sc in next 6 sc; slip st in next sc, finish off leaving an 8" (20.5 cm) length for sewing.

EAR (Make 2)

Rnd 1: With Brown, ch 4, 10 dc in fourth ch from hook; skip beginning ch and join with slip st to first dc, finish off leaving a 10" (25.5 cm) length for sewing.

FINISHING

Use photo as a guide for placement and using long ends:

- Sew Horns to Head across Rnds 17-19.
- Fold Ear in half and sew Ears to Head below Horns.
- With Black and using straight stitch *(Fig. 13, page 42)*, add x's on each side of Snout for nostrils; sew Snout to Head across Rnds 12-15.
- With Black and using satin stitch *(Fig. 14, page 42)*, add Eyes across Rnds 15 and 16, placing them 3½ to 4 stitches apart.

Adding Head Hair

Cut 36 strands of Brown, 4" (10 cm) long.

Note: To add Hair to Head, hold Cow upside down and add fringe. This will make the Hair lay flat when Body is right side up. Use stitch posts to add fringe *(Figs. 7e & f, page 41)*.

Adding strands individually, add 3 strands of fringe in from Ear down the side of Head on each side. Working across, add fringe across and down each side of Head.

TAN HIGHLAND COW PUDGIE

EASY

Finished Height: 4" (10 cm)

SHOPPING LIST

Yarn (Medium Weight) 4

[3.5 ounces, 185 yards (100 grams, 170 meters) per skein]:

- ☐ Tan - 1 skein
- ☐ Cream - 1 skein **or** 10 yards (9 meters)
- ☐ Dark Brown - 2 yards (1.8 meters)
- ☐ Pink - 1 yard (.9 meters)
- ☐ Blue - 1 yard (.9 meters)

Crochet Hook

- ☐ Size G (4 mm) **or** size needed for gauge

Additional Supplies

- ☐ Polyester fiberfill
- ☐ Yarn needle

GAUGE INFORMATION

8 sc and 9 rows/rnds = 2" (5 cm)

Gauge Swatch: 2" (5 cm) diameter

Work same as Head & Body through Rnd 4: 32 sc.

Save time, check your gauge.

HEAD & BODY

Rnd 1 (Right side)**:** With Tan and beginning at bottom of Body, make an adjustable ring, work 8 sc in ring ***(Figs. 2a-d, page 39)***; do **not** join, place marker to indicate the beginning of the round ***(Fig. 1, page 39)***.

Note: Loop a short piece of yarn around any stitch to mark Rnd 1 as **right** side.

Rnd 2: 2 Sc in each sc around: 16 sc.

Rnd 3: (Sc in next sc, 2 sc in next sc) around: 24 sc.

Rnd 4: (Sc in next 2 sc, 2 sc in next sc) around: 32 sc.

Rnd 5: (Sc in next 3 sc, 2 sc in next sc) around: 40 sc.

Rnds 6 and 7: Sc in each sc around.

Rnd 8: (Sc in next 3 sc, sc2tog) around: 32 sc.

Rnds 9 and 10: Sc in each sc around.

Rnd 11: (Sc in next 2 sc, sc2tog) around: 24 sc.

Rnds 12-15: Sc in each sc around.

Rnd 16: (Sc in next sc, sc2tog) around: 16 sc.

Rnd 17-19: Sc in each sc around.

Stuff piece with polyester fiberfill, shaping piece like an egg.

Rnd 20: Sc2tog around; slip st in next sc, finish off leaving an 8" (20.5 cm) length for sewing: 8 sts.

Thread yarn needle with end and weave yarn through Front Loop Only of remaining st to close ***(Fig. 4, page 40)***; secure end.

SNOUT

Rnd 1 (Right side)**:** With Cream, ch 4; 2 sc in second ch from hook, sc in next ch, 4 sc in last ch; workin in free loops on opposite side of ch ***(Fig. 5b, page 40)***, sc in next ch, 2 sc in next ch; join with slip st to first sc: 10 sc.

Note: Mark Rnd 1 as **right** side.

Rnd 2: Ch 1, 2 sc in same st as joining, sc in next 3 sc, 2 sc in each of next 2 sc, sc in next 3 sc, 2 sc in last sc; join with slip to first sc, finish off leaving an 8" (20.5 cm) length for sewing.

HORN (Make 2)

Rnd 1 (Right side)**:** With Cream, ch 2, 3 sc in second ch from hook; do **not** join, place marker to indicate the beginning of the round.

Note: Mark Rnd 1 as **right** side.

Rnd 2: 2 Sc in next sc, sc in next 2 sc: 4 sc.

Rnd 3: 2 Sc in next sc, sc in next 3 sc: 5 sc.

Rnd 4: 2 Sc in next sc, sc in next 4 sc: 6 sc.

Rnd 5: 2 Sc in next sc, sc in next 5 sc: 7 sc.

Rnd 6: 2 Sc in next sc, sc in next 6 sc; slip st in next sc, finish off leaving an 8" (20.5 cm) length for sewing.

EAR (Make 2)

Rnd 1: With Tan, ch 4, 10 dc in fourth ch from hook; skip beginning ch and join with slip st to first dc, finish off leaving a 10" (25.5 cm) length for sewing.

FINISHING

Use photo as a guide for placement and using long ends:

- Sew Horns to Head, across Rnds 17-19.
- Fold Ear in half and sew Ears to Head below Horns.
- With Dark Brown and using straight stitch ***(Fig. 13, page 42)***, add x's on each side of Snout; sew Snout to Head across Rnds 12-15.
- With Dark Brown and using satin stitch ***(Fig. 14, page 42)***, add Eyes across Rnds 15 and 16, placing them 3½ to 4 stitches apart.

Adding Head Hair

Cut 18 strands **each** of Tan and Cream, 4" (10 cm) long.

Note: To add Hair to Head, hold Cow upside down and add fringe. This will make the Hair lay flat when Body is right side up. Use stitch posts to add fringe ***(Figs. 7e & f, page 41)***. Alternate Cream and Tan strands throughout.

Adding strands individually, add 3 strands of fringe in from Ear down the side of Head on each side. Working across, add fringe across and down each side of Head. Fill in top of Head with fringe.

Flower

(Make 1 **each** in Pink & Blue)

Rnd 1 (Right side)**:** With color indicated, ch 3, slip st in third ch from hook, (ch 2, slip st in same ch) 4 times; finish off leaving an 8" (20.5 cm) length for sewing.

Sew Flowers to Head.

GENERAL INSTRUCTIONS

ABBREVIATIONS

ch(s)	chain(s)
cm	centimeter
dc	double crochet(s)
FPdc	Front Post double crochet(s)
FPsc	Front Post single crochet(s)
hdc	half double crochet(s)
mm	millimeters
Rnd(s)	Round(s)
sc	single crochet(s)
sc2tog	single crochet 2 together
sc3tog	single crochet 3 together
sp(s)	space(s)
st(s)	stitch(es)
YO	yarn over

SYMBOLS & TERMS

★ — work instructions following ★ as many **more** times as indicated in addition to the first time.

† to † — work all instructions from first † to second † as many times as specified.

( ) or [ ] — work enclosed instructions **as many** times as specified by the number immediately following **or** work all enclosed instructions in the stitch or space indicated **or** contains explanatory remarks.

colon (:) — the number(s) given after a colon at the end of a row or round denote(s) the number of stitches you should have on that row or round.

Yarn Weight Symbol & Names	LACE 0	SUPER FINE 1	FINE 2	LIGHT 3	MEDIUM 4	BULKY 5	SUPER BULKY 6	JUMBO 7
Type of Yarns in Category	Fingering, size 10 crochet thread	Sock, Fingering, Baby	Sport, Baby	DK, Light Worsted	Worsted, Afghan, Aran	Chunky, Craft, Rug	Super Bulky, Roving	Jumbo, Roving
Crochet Gauge* Ranges in Single Crochet to 4" (10 cm)	32-42 sts**	21-32 sts	16-20 sts	12-17 sts	11-14 sts	8-11 sts	6-9 sts	5 sts and fewer
Advised Hook Size Range	Steel*** 6 to 8, Regular hook B-1	B-1 to E-4	E-4 to 7	7 to I-9	I-9 to K-10½	K-10½ to M/N-13	M/N-13 to Q	Q and larger

*GUIDELINES ONLY: The chart above reflects the most commonly used gauges and hook sizes for specific yarn categories.

** Lace weight yarns are usually crocheted with larger hooks to create lacy openwork patterns. Accordingly, a gauge range is difficult to determine. Always follow the gauge stated in your pattern.

*** Steel crochet hooks are sized differently from regular hooks–the higher the number, the smaller the hook, which is the reverse of regular hook sizing.

CROCHET TERMINOLOGY		
UNITED STATES		INTERNATIONAL
slip stitch (slip st)	=	single crochet (sc)
single crochet (sc)	=	double crochet (dc)
half double crochet (hdc)	=	half treble crochet (htr)
double crochet (dc)	=	treble crochet (tr)
treble crochet (tr)	=	double treble crochet (dtr)
double treble crochet (dtr)	=	triple treble crochet (ttr)
triple treble crochet (tr tr)	=	quadruple treble crochet (qtr)
skip	=	miss

BASIC	Projects using basic stitches. May include basic increases and decreases.
EASY	Projects may include simple stitch patterns, color work, and/or shaping.
INTERMEDIATE	Projects may include involved stitch patterns, color work, and/or shaping.
COMPLEX	Projects may include complex stitch patterns, color work, and/or shaping using a variety of techniques and stitches simultaneously.

CROCHET HOOKS																	
U.S.	B-1	C-2	D-3	E-4	F-5	G-6	7	H-8	I-9	J-10	K-10½	L-11	M/N-13	N/P-15	P/Q	Q	S
Metric - mm	2.25	2.75	3.25	3.5	3.75	4	4.5	5	5.5	6	6.5	8	9	10	15	16	19

GAUGE

Exact gauge is essential for proper size. Before beginning your project, make the sample swatch given in the individual instructions in the yarn and hook specified. After completing the swatch, measure it, counting your stitches and rows/rounds carefully. If your swatch is larger or smaller than specified, **make another, changing hook size to get the correct gauge**. Keep trying until you find the size hook that will give you the specified gauge.

MARKERS

Markers are used to help distinguish the beginning of each round being worked. Place a 2" (5 cm) scrap piece of yarn before the first stitch of each round, moving markers after each round is complete.

Fig. 1

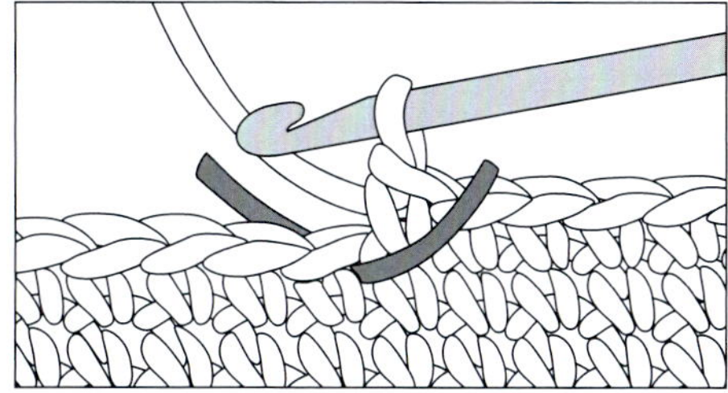

ADJUSTABLE RING

Wind the yarn around two fingers to form a ring ***(Fig. 2a)***.

Slide the yarn off your fingers and grasp the strands at the top of the ring ***(Fig. 2b)***.

Insert the hook from front to back into the ring, pull up a loop, YO and draw through the loop on hook to lock the ring ***(Fig. 2c)***.

Working around both strands, work stitches in the ring as specified, then pull the end to close ***(Fig. 2d)***.

Fig. 2a

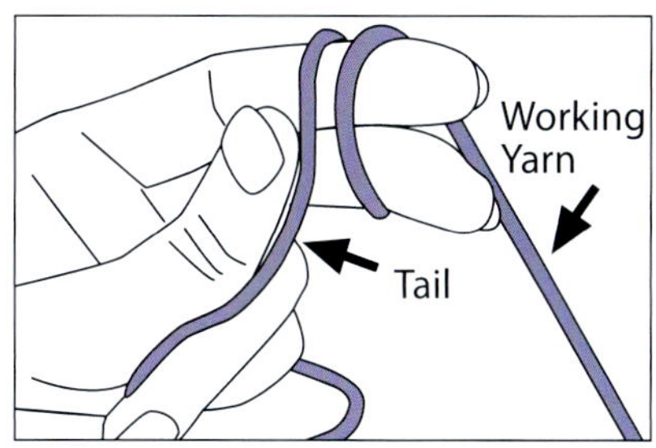

Fig. 2b

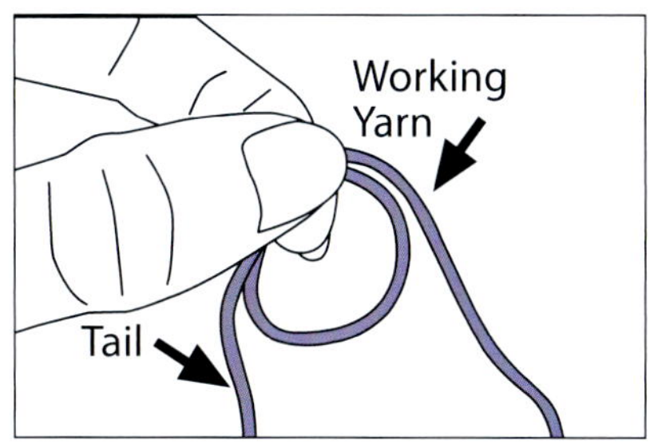

Fig. 2c

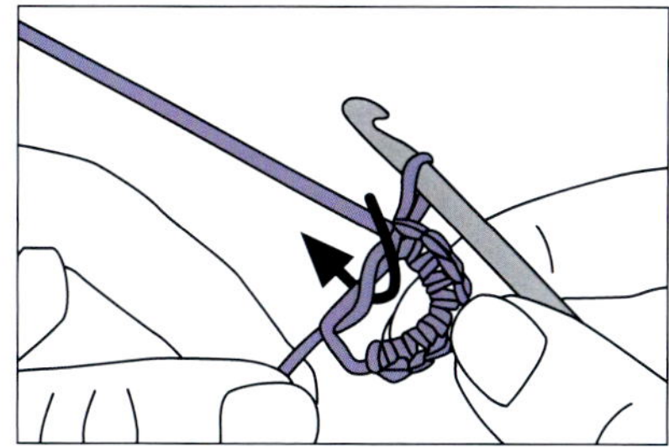

Fig. 2d

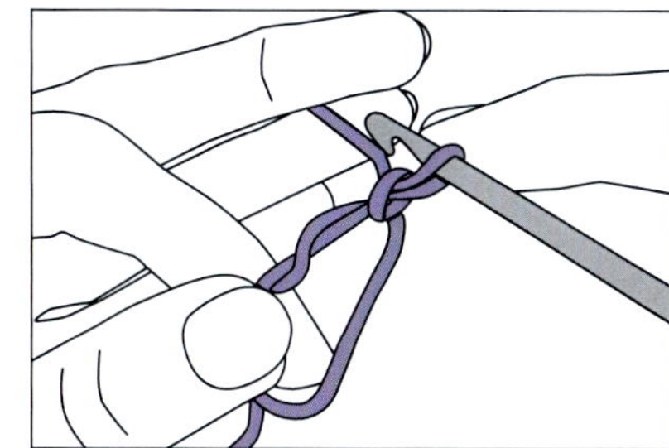

BACK RIDGE OF A CHAIN

Work in loops indicated by arrows *(Fig. 3)*.

Fig. 3

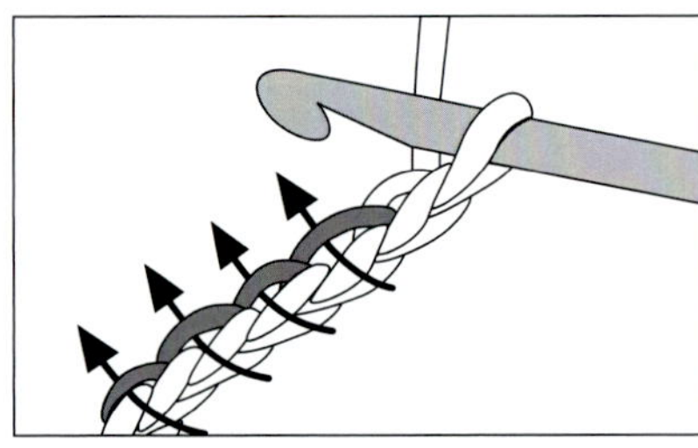

BACK OR FRONT LOOPS ONLY

Work only in loop(s) indicated by arrow *(Fig. 4)*.

Fig. 4

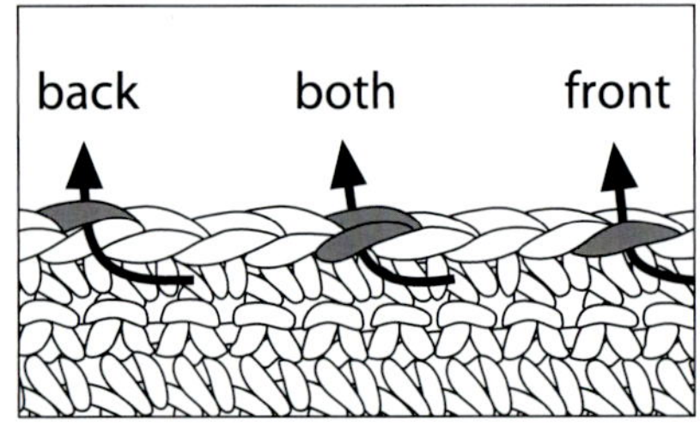

FREE LOOPS

After working in Back or Front Loops Only on a row or round, there will be a ridge of unused loops. These are called the free loops. Later, when instructed to work in the free loops of the same row or round, work in these loops *(Fig. 5a)*.

Fig. 5a

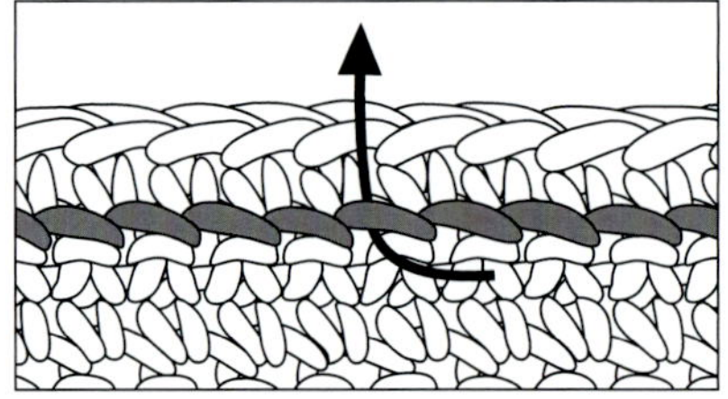

When instructed to work in free loops of a chain, work in loop indicated by arrow *(Fig. 5b)*.

Fig. 5b

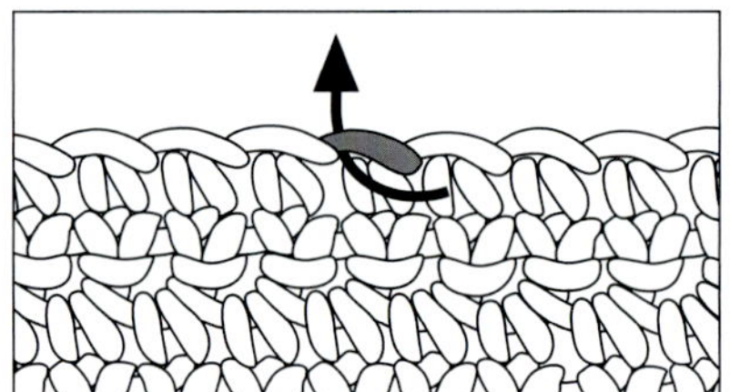

ATTACHING SAFETY EYES

Centering eyes on stuffed head, insert post of eye, from right side, between rounds indicated. Remove fiber-fill as needed. From the wrong side, place plastic washer on post and push onto post until washer is flush with crochet fabric. Replace fiberfill.

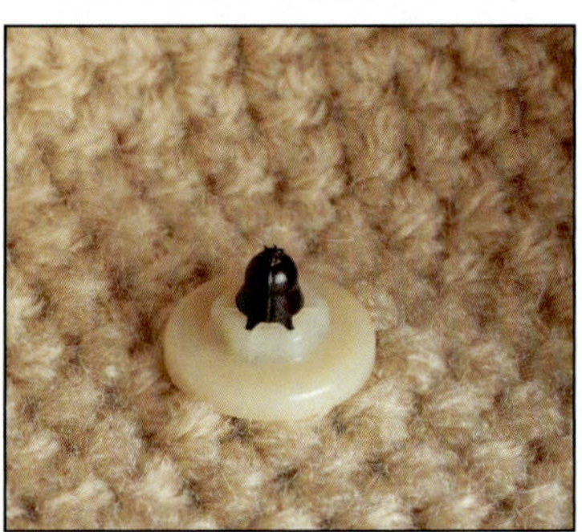

SURFACE SLIP STITCH

Begin with a slip knot and place it behind the crocheted fabric (on the **wrong** side). Working as instructed in individual instructions, insert hook into fabric from **front** to **back** and place the slip knot on the hook, pull loop through fabric to the **right** side. ★ Keeping the working yarn **behind** the fabric, insert hook into fabric from **front** to **back** and yarn over with the working yarn, pull the loop through the fabric to the **right** side **AND** through the loop on the front of the fabric; repeat from ★ for each stitch.

WHIPSTITCH

Place two Motifs with **wrong** sides together and as instructed in individual instructions. Beginning in center stitch of corner, sew through both pieces once to secure the beginning of the seam, leaving an ample yarn end to weave in later. Insert the needle from **front** to **back** through **both** loops on **both** pieces. Bring the needle around and insert it from **front** to **back** through the next loops of **both** pieces *(Fig. 6)*. Continue in this manner across to center stitch of next corner, keeping the sewing yarn fairly loose.

Fig. 6

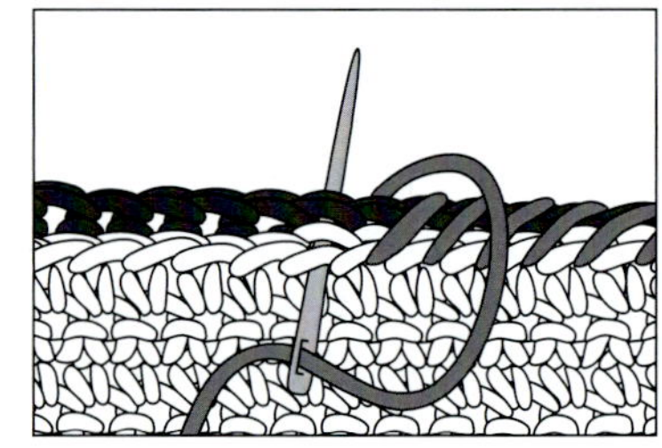

FRINGE

ADDING FRINGE IN END OF ROWS

Fold strands in half. With **wrong** side facing and using crochet hook, draw the folded end up through end of row and pull the loose ends through the folded end ***(Fig. 7a)***; draw the knot up tightly ***(Fig. 7b)***. Repeat in end of each row indicated. Trim ends evenly.

Fig. 7a

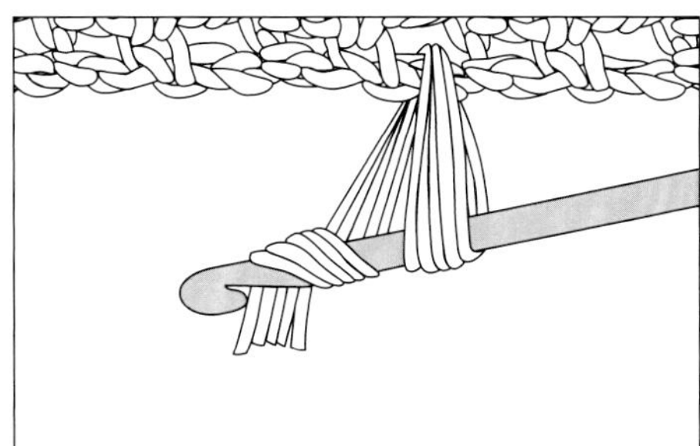

Fig. 7b

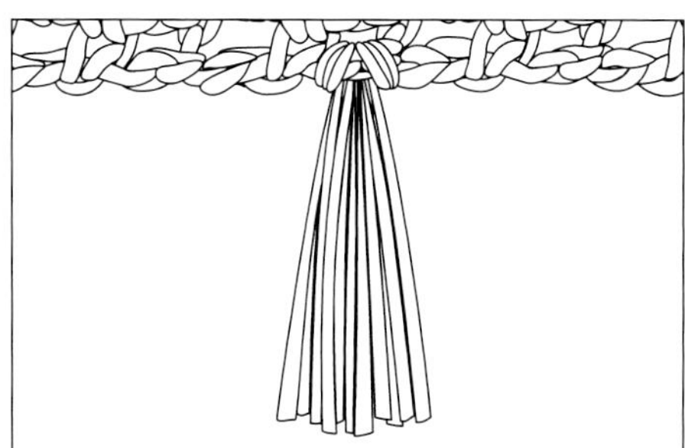

ADDING FRINGE IN FREE LOOPS

Fold strand in half. Using a crochet hook, draw the folded end through a free loop and pull the loose ends through the folded end ***(Fig. 7c)***; draw the knot up tightly ***(Fig. 7d)***. Repeat in each free loop. Trim ends evenly.

Fig. 7c

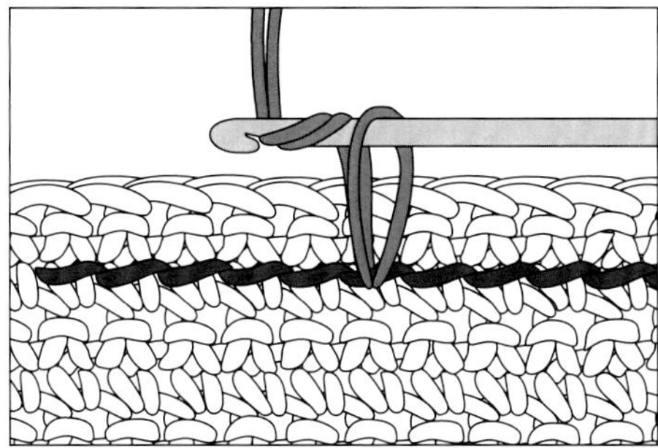

Fig. 7d

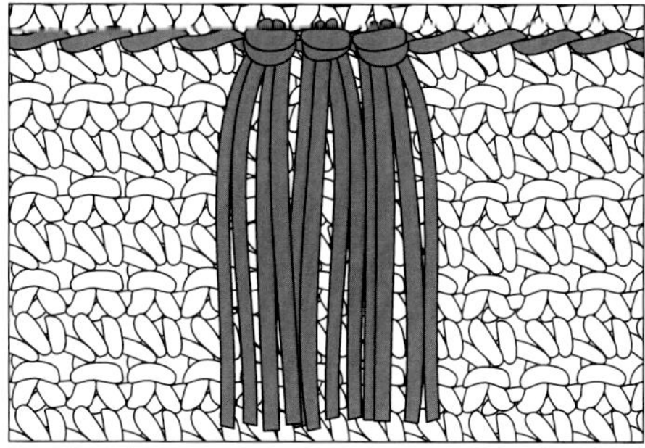

ADDING FRINGE AROUND STITCH POSTS

Fold strand in half. Using a crochet hook, insert the hook from **front** to **back** to **front** again around post of stitch, draw the folded end through and pull the loose ends through the folded end; draw the knot up tightly. Repeat around desired stitch posts. Trim ends as desired.

Fig. 7e

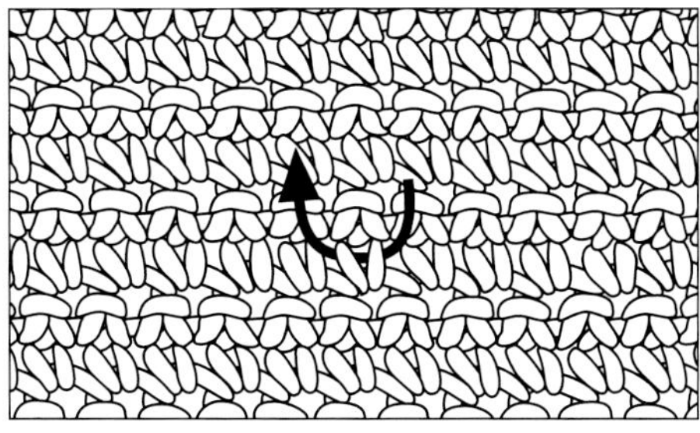

Fig. 7f

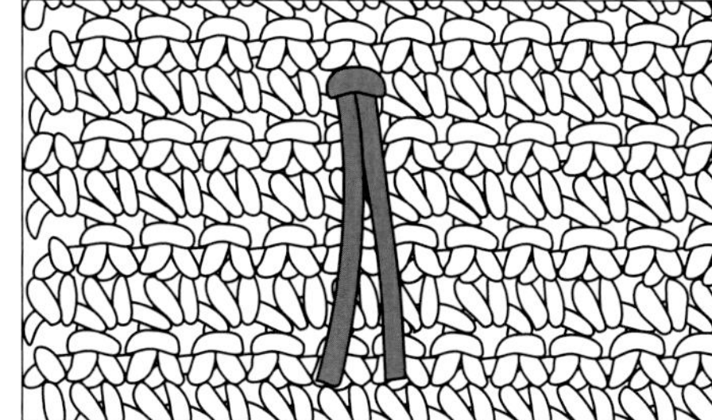

BASIC CROCHET STITCHES

SLIP STITCH

Insert hook in stitch indicated, YO and draw through stitch and through loop on hook ***(Fig. 8) (abbreviated slip st)***.

Fig. 8

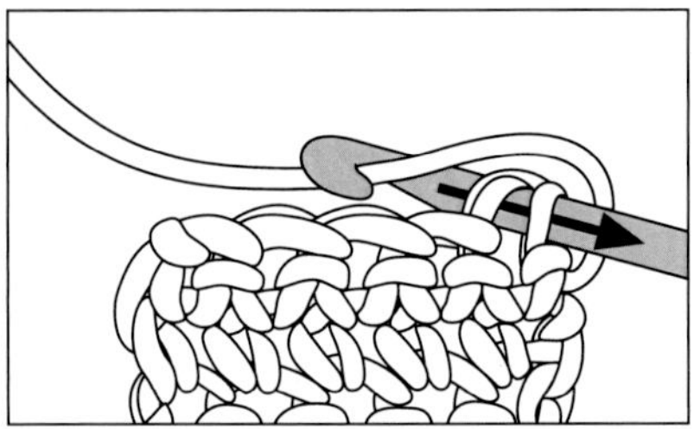

SINGLE CROCHET

Insert hook in stitch indicated, YO and pull up a loop, YO and draw through both loops on hook ***(Fig. 9) (abbreviated sc)***.

Fig. 9

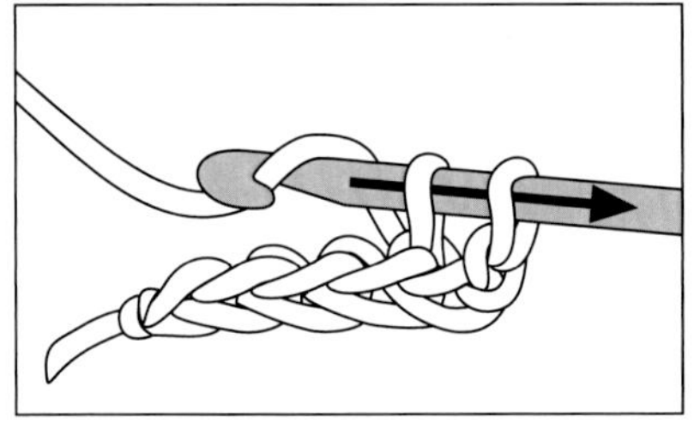

HALF DOUBLE CROCHET

YO, insert hook in stitch indicated, YO and pull up a loop, YO and draw through all 3 loops on hook ***(Fig. 10) (abbreviated hdc)***.

Fig. 10

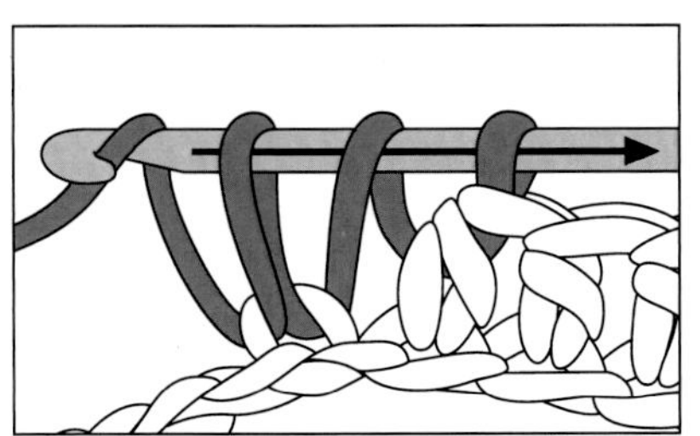

DOUBLE CROCHET

YO, insert hook in stitch indicated, YO and pull up a loop (3 loops on hook), YO and draw through 2 loops on hook ***(Fig. 11a)***, YO and draw through remaining 2 loops on hook ***(Fig. 11b) (abbreviated dc)***.

Fig. 11a

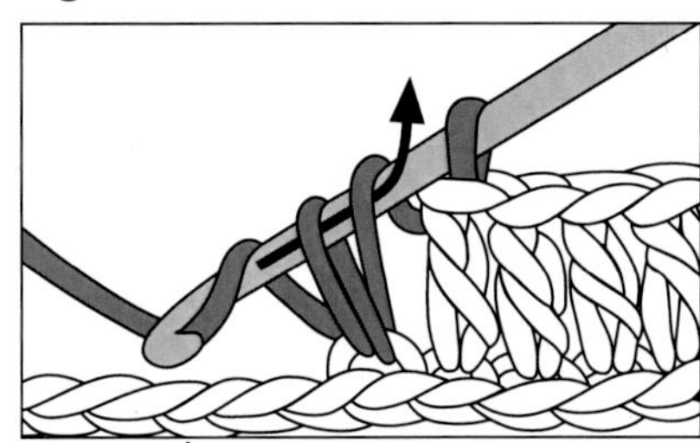

Fig. 11b

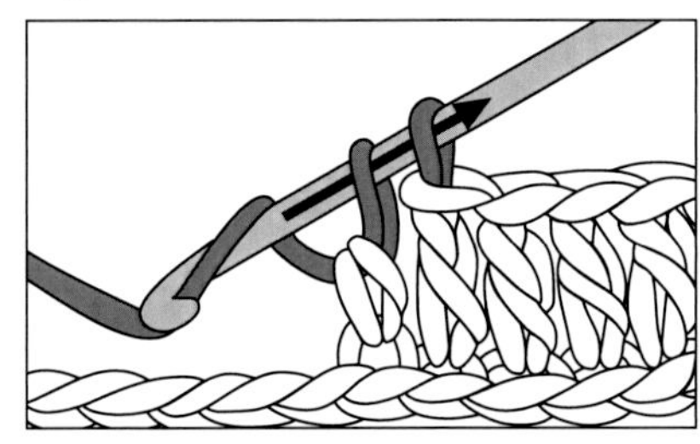

TREBLE CROCHET

YO twice, insert hook in stitch indicated, YO and pull up a loop (4 loops on hook) ***(Fig. 12a)***, (YO and draw through 2 loops on hook) 3 times ***(Fig. 12b) (abbreviated tr)***.

Fig. 12a

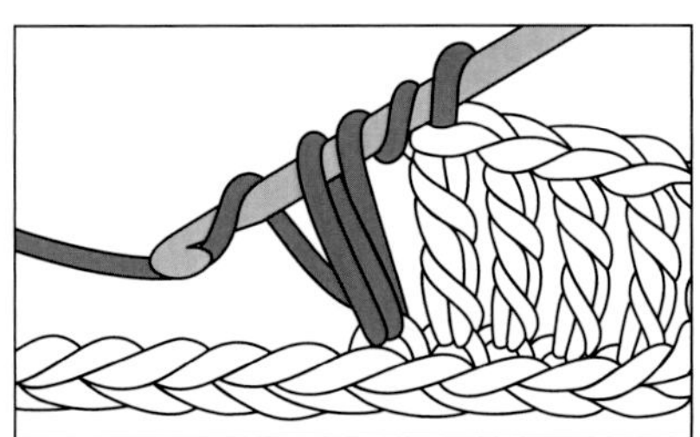

Fig. 12b

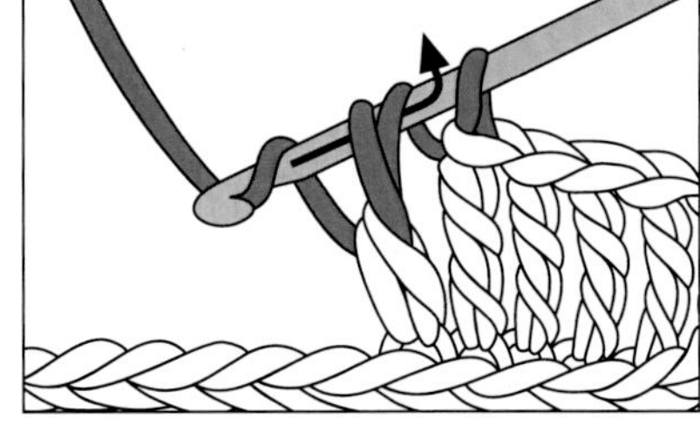

EMBROIDERY STITCHES

STRAIGHT STITCH

Straight Stitch is just what the name implies, a single, straight stitch. Come up at 1 and go down at 2 ***(Fig. 13)***.

Fig. 13

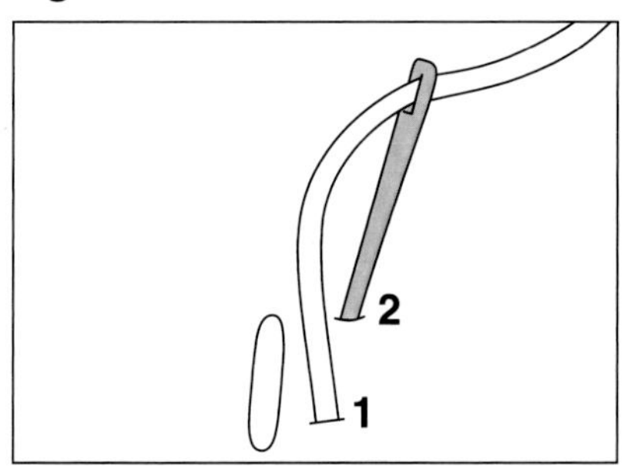

SATIN STITCH

Satin stitch is a series of straight stitches worked side-by-side, so they touch but do not overlap. Come up at odd numbers and go down at even numbers ***(Fig. 9)***.

Fig. 14

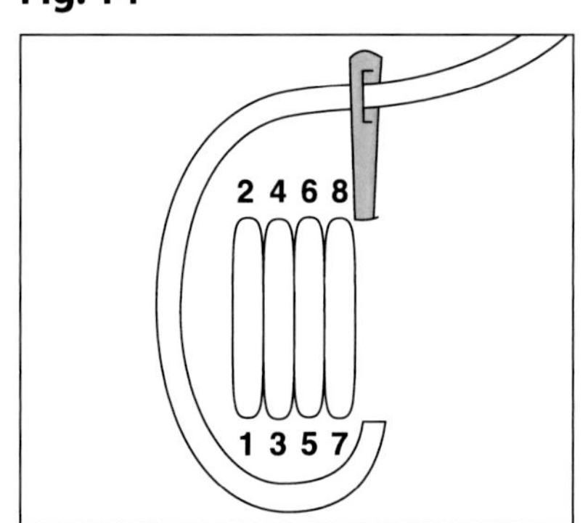

YARN INFORMATION

The projects in this book were made using a Medium Weight yarn. Any brand of Medium Weight yarn may be used. It is best to refer to the yardage/meters when determining how many balls or skeins to purchase. Remember to achieve the same look, it is the weight of yarn that is important, not the brand of yarn.

For your convenience, listed below are the specific yarns used to create our photography models. Because yarn manufacturers make frequent changes to their product lines, you may sometimes find it necessary to use a substitute yarn or to search for the discontinued product at alternate suppliers (locally or online).

HIGHLAND COW
Lion Brand®
Basic Stitch Anti-Pilling™ Yarn
Main Color (Brown) - #125AA Truffle
Dark Brown - #128E Ebony
Cream - #410F Beige Heather

BLANKET
Lion Brand®
Basic Stitch Anti-Pilling™ Yarn
Taupe - #402K Taupe Heather
Gold - #134U Honey
Tan - #121L Almond
Brown - #125AA Truffle
Dark Brown - #128E Ebony
Cream - #410F Beige Heather
Pink - #101F Baby Pink

HIGHLAND COW PUDGIE
Lion Brand®
Basic Stitch Anti-Pilling™ Yarn
Brown - #125AA Truffle
Cream - #410F Beige Heather
Black - #153 Black

TAN HIGHLAND COW
Lion Brand®
Basic Stitch Anti-Pilling™ Yarn
Main Color (Tan) - #121L Almond
Dark Brown - #128E Ebony
Cream - #410F Beige Heather

PILLOW
Lion Brand®
Basic Stitch Anti-Pilling™ Yarn
Taupe - #402K Taupe Heather
Gold - #134U Honey
Tan - #121L Almond
Brown - #125AA Truffle
Dark Brown - #128 E Ebony
Cream - #410F Beige Heather
Pink - #101F Baby Pink

TAN HIGHLAND COW PUDGIE
Lion Brand®
Basic Stitch Anti-Pilling™ Yarn
Tan - #121L Almond
Cream - #410F Beige Heather
Dark Brown - #128E Ebony
Pink - #101F Baby Pink
Blue - #106A Baby Blue

Photo models made and instructions tested by Lizzy Griffin,
Vicky Heimbecker, and Abbie Johnson.

Production Team:
Designer – Kristi Simpson;
Creative Director – Mimi Wardlaw;
Assistant Art Director – Toni Kerr;
Technical Editor – Linda A. Daley & Kristi Simpson;
Editorial Editor – Shelbey Winningham;
Graphic Artist – Christine DeLillo;
Photo Stylist – Kelly Huffman;
Photographer – Rob Karman.

Made in U.S.A.